KOREAN

Made Nice & Easy!™

Staff of Research & Education Association
Carl Fuchs, Language Program Director

Based on Language Courses developed by the
U.S. Government for Foreign Service Personnel

Research & Education Association
61 Ethel Road West
Piscataway, New Jersey 08854

Dr. M. Fogiel, Director

KOREAN MADE NICE & EASY™

Printed in the United States of America

Library of Congress Control Number 00-193029

International Standard Book Number 0-87891-373-4

LANGUAGES MADE NICE & EASY is a trademark of Research & Education Association, Piscataway, New Jersey 08854

What This Guide Will Do For You

Whether travelling to a foreign country or to your favorite international restaurant, this *Nice & Easy* guide gives you just enough of the language to get around and be understood. Much of the material in this book was developed for government personnel who are often assigned to a foreign country on a moment's notice and need a quick introduction to the language.

In this handy and compact guide, you will find useful words and phrases, popular expressions, common greetings, and the words for numbers, money, and time. Every word or phrase is accompanied with the correct pronunciation. There is a vocabulary list for finding words quickly.

Generous margins on the pages allow you to make notes and remarks that you may find helpful.

If you expect to travel to Korea, the section on the country's history and relevant up-to-date facts will make your trip more informative and enjoyable. By keeping this guide with you, you'll be well prepared to understand as well as converse in Korean.

Carl Fuchs
Language Program Director

Contents

Korean Facts and History v

Hints on Pronunciation 7

Special Points 9

Useful Words and Phrases 12

Greetings and General Phrases 12

Location 14

Directions 15

Numbers 18

What's This? 22

Asking For Things 22

Money 24

Time 25

Other Useful Phrases 28

Additional Expressions 29

Fill-In Sentences 34

Expressions with Numbers 43

Important Signs 47

Vocabulary List 51

SOUTH KOREA

Facts & History

Official Name: Republic of Korea

Geography

Area: 98,500 sq. km. (38,000 sq. mi.); about the size of Indiana.

Cities: *Capital*—Seoul (11 million). *Other major cities*—Pusan (3.9 million), Taegu (2.5 million), Inchon (2.4 million), Kwangju (1.4 million), Taejon (1.3 million).

Terrain: Partially forested mountain ranges separated by deep, narrow valleys; cultivated plains along the coasts, particularly in the west and south.

Climate: Temperate.

People

Nationality: Korean(s).
Population: 46.9 million.
Annual growth rate: 1.02%.
Ethnic groups: Korean; small Chinese minority.
Religions: Christianity, Buddhism, Shamanism, Confucianism, Chondogyo.
Language: Korean.
Education: *Years compulsory*—9. *Enrollment*—11.5 million. *Attendance*—middle school 99%, high school 95%. *Literacy*—98%.
Life expectancy - men 70.1 yrs.; women 77.7 yrs.
Work force: 21.5 million. *Services*—61%; *mining and manufacturing*—24%; *agriculture*—15%.

Government

Type: Republic with powers shared between the president and the legislature.
Liberation: August 15, 1945.
Constitution: July 17, 1948; last revised 1987.
Branches: *Executive*—president (chief of state). *Legislative*—unicameral National Assembly. *Judicial*—Supreme Court and appellate courts; Constitutional Court.

Economy

GDP: Approximately $406.7 billion.
Natural resources: Limited coal, tungsten, iron ore,

limestone, kaolinite, and graphite.
Agriculture (including forestry and fisheries): *Products*—rice, vegetables, fruit. *Arable land*—22% of land area.
Mining and manufacturing: Textiles, footwear, electronics and electrical equipment, shipbuilding, motor vehicles, petrochemicals, industrial machinery. Trade : *Exports*—$143.7 billion: manufactures, textiles, ships, automobiles, steel, computers, footwear. *Major markets*—U.S., Japan, ASEAN, European Union. *Imports*—$119.7 billion: crude oil, food, machinery and transportation equipment, chemicals and chemical products, base metals and articles. *Major suppliers*—Japan, U.S., European Union, Middle East.

People

The origins of the Korean people are obscure. Korea was first populated by a people or peoples who migrated to the peninsula from the northwestern regions of Asia, some of whom also settled parts of northeast China (Manchuria). Koreans are racially and linguistically homogeneous, with no sizable indigenous minorities, except for some Chinese (about 20,000).

South Korea's major population centers are in the northwest area and in the fertile plain to the south of

Seoul-Inchon. The mountainous central and eastern areas are sparsely inhabited. The Japanese colonial administration of 1910-45 concentrated its industrial development efforts in the comparatively under-populated and resource-rich north, resulting in a considerable migration of people to the north from the southern agrarian provinces. This trend was reversed after World War II as Koreans returned to the south from Japan and Manchuria. In addition, more than 2 million Koreans moved to the south from the north following the division of the peninsula into U.S. and Soviet military zones of administration in 1945. This migration continued after the Republic of Korea was established in 1948 and during the Korean war (1950-53). About 10% of the people now in the Republic of Korea are of northern origin. With 46 million people, South Korea has one of the world's highest population densities—much higher, for example, than India or Japan—while the territorially larger North Korea has only about 22 million people. Ethnic Koreans now residing in other countries live mostly in China (1.9 million), the United States (1.52 million), Japan (681,000), and the countries of the former Soviet Union (450,000).

Language

The Korean language shares several grammatical features with Japanese, and there are strong similarities with Mongolian, but the exact relationship among these three languages is unclear. Although regional dialects exist, the language spoken throughout the peninsula and in China is comprehensible by all Koreans. Chinese characters were used to write Korean before the Korean Hangul alphabet was invented in the 15th century. Chinese characters are still in limited use in South Korea, but the North uses Hangul exclusively. Many older people retain some knowledge of Japanese from the colonial period, and many educated South Koreans can speak and/or read English, which is taught in all secondary schools.

Religion

Korea's traditional religions are Buddhism and Shamanism. Buddhism has lost some influence over the years but is still followed by about 27% of the population. Shamanism—traditional spirit worship—is still practiced. Confucianism remains a dominant cultural influence. Since the Japanese occupation, it has existed more as a shared base than as a separate philosophical/religious school. Some sources place the number of adherents of Chondogyo—a native religion founded in the mid-19th century that fuses elements of Confucianism and Christianity—at more than 1 million.

Christian missionaries arrived in Korea as early as

the 16th century, but it was not until the 19th century that they founded schools, hospitals, and other modern institutions throughout the country. Christianity is now one of Korea's largest religions. In 1993, nearly 10.5 million Koreans, or 24% of the population, were Christians (about 76% of them Protestant)—the largest figure for any East Asian country, except the Philippines.

History of Korea

According to Korean legend, the god-king Tangun founded the Korean nation in BC 2333. By the first century AD, the Korean Peninsula was divided into the kingdoms of Silla, Koguryo, and Paekche. The Silla kingdom unified the peninsula in 668 AD. The Koryo dynasty (from which the Western name "Korea" is derived) succeeded the Silla kingdom in 935. The Choson dynasty, ruled by members of the Yi clan, supplanted Koryo in 1392 and lasted until the Japanese annexed Korea in 1910.

Throughout most of its history, Korea has been invaded, influenced, and fought over by its larger neighbors. It has suffered approximately 900 invasions during its 2,000 years of recorded history. Korea was under Mongolian occupation from 1231 until the early 14th century and was repeatedly ravaged by Chinese (government and rebel) armies. The Japanese warlord Hideyoshi launched major invasions in 1592 and 1597. China had by far the greatest influence of the major powers and was the most acceptable to the Koreans. The Choson Dynasty was part of the Chinese "tribute" system, under which Korea was independent in fact but acknowledged China's theoretical role as "big brother." China was the only exception to Korea's long closed-door policy, adopted to ward off foreign encroachment, which earned it the name of "Hermit Kingdom" in the 19th century. Korea's isolation finally ended when the major Western powers and Japan sent warships to forcibly open the country. At the same time, Japanese, Chinese, and Russian competition in Northeast Asia led to armed conflict, and foreign intervention established dominance in Korea, formally annexing it in 1910.

The Japanese colonial era was characterized by tight control from Tokyo and ruthless efforts to supplant Korean language and culture. Organized Korean resistance, notably the 1919 Independence Movement, was unsuccessful, and Japan remained firmly in control until the end of World War II. Near the end of the war, the April 1945 Yalta Conference agreed to establish a four-power trusteeship for Korea. The trusteeship of the U.S., U.K., Soviet Union, and China was intended as a temporary administrative measure pending democratic elections for a Korean Government. With the unexpected early surrender of Japan in September 1945, the United States proposed—and the Soviet Union agreed—that Japanese troops surrender to U.S. forces below the 38th parallel and to Soviet forces above.

At a December 1945 foreign ministers' conference in Moscow, it was proposed that a 5-year trusteeship be established in Korea. The U.S. submitted the Korean question to the UN General Assembly for resolution in September 1947. In November, the General Assembly ruled that UN-supervised elections should be held. The Soviet Union and Korean authorities in the North ignored the UN General Assembly resolution on elections. Nonetheless, elections were carried out under UN observation in the South, and on August 15, 1948, the Republic of Korea (R.O.K.) was established. Syngman Rhee became the Republic of Korea's first president. On September 9, 1948, the Democratic People's Republic of Korea (D.P.R.K.) was established in the North under Kim Il Sung. Both administrations claimed to be the only legitimate government on the peninsula.

Korean War of 1950-53

On June 25, 1950, North Korean forces invaded South Korea. The UN, in accord with its Charter, engaged in its first collective action by establishing the UN Command (UNC), under which 16 member nations sent troops and assistance to South Korea. At the request of the UN Security Council, the United States, contributor of the largest contingent, led this international effort.

Although armistice negotiations began in July 1951, hostilities continued until 1953 with heavy losses on both sides. On July 27, 1953 the military commanders of the North Korean Army, the Chinese People's Volunteers, and the UNC signed an armistice agreement at Panmunjom. Neither the United States nor South Korea is a signatory of the armistice per se, though both adhere to it through the UNC. No comprehensive peace agreement has replaced the 1953 armistice pact; thus, a condition of belligerency still technically exists on the divided peninsula.

Toward Democratization

Syngman Rhee served as president of the Republic of Korea until April 1960, when unrest led by university students forced him to step down. Though the constitution was amended and national elections were held in June, Maj. Gen. Park Chung Hee led an army coup against the successor government and assumed power in May 1961. After 2 years of military government under Park, civilian rule was restored in 1963. Park, who had retired from the army, was elected president and was reelected in 1967, 1971, and 1978 in highly controversial elections.

The Park era, marked by rapid industrial modernization and extraordinary economic growth, ended with his assassination in October 1979. In December 1979 Maj. Gen. Chun Doo Hwan and close military colleagues staged a coup, removing the army chief of staff and soon effectively controlling the government. Though martial law ended in January 1981, his government retained broad legal powers to control dissent. In June 1987, the ruling party presidential candidate Roh Tae Woo announced the implementation of democratic reforms. The constitution was revised in October 1987 to include direct presidential elections and a strengthened National Assembly consisting of 299 members. The new constitution entered into force in February 1988 when President Roh assumed office.

In April 1996, Presidents Clinton and Kim invited the D.P.R.K. and the People's Republic of China to participate in four-party peace talks on the future of the Korean Peninsula. The four parties focused their efforts on achieving progress on tension reduction in the Korean Peninsula and the establishment of a permanent peace regime there that would replace the 1953 military armistice.

Kangwon-Do - Chorwon

Kyongsangbuk-Do - Pagoda At Kamunsa

Kyongju - Pulguk-Sa - Pulguk Temple

Kyonggi-Do - Suchong Temple On Wungil Mountain

Farmer's Dance At Korean Folk Village

Kyongju - Pulguk-Sa (Pulguk Temple)

Hints on Pronunciation

All the words and phrases are written in a spelling which you read like English. Each letter or combination of letters is used for the sound it normally represents in English and it *always* stands for the same sound. Thus, "oo" is always to be read as in *too, boot, tooth, roost,* never as in *blood* or *door.* Say these words and then pronounce the vowel sound by itself. That is the sound you must use every time you see "oo" in the PRONUNCIATION column. If you should use some other sound—for example, the one in *blood* or the one in *door*—you might be misunderstood.

Syllables that are accented—that is, pronounced louder than others—are written in capital letters. Apostrophes (') are used to show sounds that are pronounced together without any break; for ex-

Kyongbokkung - Kyongbuk Palace

Temple In Soraksan National Park

8

ample, "AHN-n'yung" in the expression "AHN-n'yung hah-SIM-nik-gah?" meaning "How do you do?"

Special Points

Here are a few points to remember as you read the PRONUNCIATION column:

AH   as in *father, bah, ah.* Example: "SAH" meaning "four."

A   as in *at, fat, hat.* Example: "NÄ-il" meaning "tomorrow."

U *or* UH   as in *huh, sun, but.* Example: "SOO-juh" meaning "eating utensils."

ER   for a sound something like the *er* in *her* or the *ur* in *hurt.* Example: "ERN" meaning "left side."

View Of Seoul

Kyonggi-Do, Namhansansong (South Han Fortress)

<u>OO</u>	when underlined, stands for a sound we don't have in English. It is like the *oo* of *book* pronounced with the lips spread apart as though about to say the *i* of *pit*. Example: "S<u>OO</u>-mool" meaning "twenty."
P, T, CH, K	in italics, stand for sounds much like those we have in *push, ten, choose, keen,* but said with a stronger rush of breath than the English sounds have. They may seem to be followed by an *h*-sound. Example: "*KAWNG*" meaning "beans."
Ḅ, Ḍ, Ģ, Ĵ, Ṣ	with dots underneath, stand for the sounds of *bake, dig, jug, go, some,* said with the throat muscles tightened. Example: "ḄAHL-lee" meaning "quickly."

Painting In Paengnyon Temple

USEFUL WORDS AND PHRASES
GREETINGS AND GENERAL PHRASES

When you are first introduced to a stranger you say:

English	Pronunciation
I greet you for the first time	*CH*UH-oom perp-S<u>OO</u>M-nee-dah
How do you do?	AHN-n'yung hah-SIM-nik-gah?

For "Good morning" you say really:

Have you had a good rest?	AHN-n'yung-hee choo-moo-suss-S<u>OO</u>M-nik-gah?

For "Good evening" you really say:

Have you had your evening meal?	*CH*UN-yuk chahp-soo-suss-S<u>OO</u>M-nik-gah?
Sir *or* Mr.	SUN-sang
Madam *or* Mrs.	POO-in
Miss	YAHNG

A *as in* at; AH *as in* bah

12

When used with proper names, these terms of address follow the noun.

Please excuse me	YAWNG-suh hah-SIP-see-yaw

When you approach a stranger on the street and want to ask for some information, it is polite to start by saying:

May I ask you a question?	MAHL-ṣoom CHAWM MOO-ruh PAWP-see-dah

In this expression is a sound you must practice. It is written "oo" with a line underneath. You heard it in the first word of the last expression. Listen again and repeat: "MAHL-soom, MAHL-soom." It is like the *oo* of *book* pronounced with the lips spread apart as though about to say the *i* of *pit*. Try just the sound again: "oo, oo."

Thank you	kaw-mahp-SOOM-nee-dah
Don't mention it	*CH*UN-mah-nay mahl-ṣoo-MIM-nee-dah

U *or* UH *as in* but

English	Pronunciation
Do you understand me?	AH-rah t<u>oo</u>k-gess-S<u>OO</u>M-nik-gah?
Yes	YAY
I understand	AH-rah t<u>oo</u>k-gess-S<u>OO</u>M-nee-dah
No	AH-nee-yaw
I don't understand	CHAHL maw-r<u>oo</u>-gess-S<u>OO</u>M-nee-dah
Please speak slowly	CHAWM *CH*UN-*ch*un-hee MAHL-ṣ<u>oo</u>m hah-SIP-see-yaw
Please repeat	CHAWM TAH-see MAHL-ṣ<u>oo</u>m hah-SIP-see-yaw

LOCATION

When you need directions to get somewhere, you first name the place and then add the phrase "Where is?"

Where is __?	__ UDD-ay iss-S<u>OO</u>M-nik-gah?
a restaurant	<u>OO</u>M-sik-jum
Where is a restaurant?	<u>oo</u>m-SIK-jum-<u>oo</u>n UDD-ay iss-S<u>OO</u>M-nik-gah?

A *as in* at; AH *as in* bah

English	Pronunciation
a hotel	YUG-wahn
Where is a hotel?	YUG-wahn-oon UDD-ay iss-SOOM-nik-gah?
the railroad station	CHUNG-guh CHAHNG
Where is the railroad station?	CHUNG-guh CHAHNG-oon UDD-ay iss-SOOM-nik-gah?
a toilet	P'YUN-saw
Where is a toilet?	P'YUN-saw-noon UDD-ay iss-SOOM-nik-gah?

DIRECTIONS

The answer to your question "Where is such-and-such?" may be "It's to the right" or "It's to the left" or "Go straight ahead," so you need to know these phrases.

Piwon (Secret Garden) In Changdokkung

15

Kyongsangbuk-Do: Toson Sowon, A Historic School Near Andong

English	*Pronunciation*
It's to the right	PAH-roon JAW-gay iss-SOOM-nee-dah
It's to the left	ERN JAW-gay iss-SOOM-nee-dah
Go straight ahead	AHP-hoo-raw KAWT-jahng kah-SIP-see-yaw

Here in these expressions are examples of another sound you must practice. It is written "j" (with the dot under it). Listen again and repeat: "JAW-gay, JAW-gay." It is like the *j* of *judge,* but you tighten your throat hard as you say it, as though you were just about to hold your breath. You will find the dot under "b," "d," "g," and "s" too, and it represents the same tightening of the throat there. Try this sound with and without this tightening of the throat. First without the tightening: "CHAW, CHAW." And with the tightening: "JAW, JAW."

Go this way	EE-ree kah-SIP-see-yaw
Please point	CHAWM KAH-rooch-huh choo-SIP-see-yaw

If you are driving and ask the distance to another town, it will be given to you in terms of Chinese miles.

Chinese mile   EE

> [NOTE: This word changes its form when numbers are added to make combinations like "two miles," "three miles," etc. See pages 43-45.]

One Chinese mile is about one-third of an English mile.

Kyongsangbuk-Do - Hahoe Traditional Village

NUMBERS

There are two sets of words in Korean for numbers less than one hundred, and both are used often. One is the native Korean system, and the other is borrowed from Chinese. In the native Korean system, the numbers are as follows:

One	HAH-nah
Two	TOOL
Three	SET
Four	NET
Five	TAH-sut
Six	YUSS-ut
Seven	IL-gawp
Eight	YUD-ul
Nine	AH-hawp
Ten	YUL

For "eleven" through "nineteen" you simply say the word for "ten" followed by the word for "one," "two," "three," etc. For example:

Fifteen	YUL-ḑah-sut
Twenty	SOO-mool

A *as in* at; AH *as in* bah

Pusan Harbor

English	Pronunciation
Thirty	SUH-r<u>oo</u>n
Forty	MAH-h<u>oo</u>n
Fifty	SHWIN
Sixty	YAY-shwin
Seventy	EE-r<u>oo</u>n
Eighty	YUD-<u>oo</u>n
Ninety	AH-h<u>oo</u>n

Numbers like "twenty-one," "thirty-five," etc., are put together just as in English. For example:

Twenty-one	S<u>OO</u>-mool HAH-nah

In the system borrowed from Chinese, the numbers are:

One	IL
Two	EE
Three	SAHM
Four	SAH
Five	AW
Six	YOOK
Seven	*CH*IL
Eight	*PAHL*

A *as in* at; AH *as in* bah

English	Pronunciation
Nine	KOO
Ten	SIP

In this system, too, the numbers from "eleven" through "nineteen" are made by saying the word for "ten" followed by the word for "one," "two," etc. Numbers like "twenty-one," "thirty-five," etc., are put together just as in English, and as in the native Korean system.

In the Chinese system the numbers "twenty," "thirty," etc. up through "ninety," are made by saying "two ten," "three ten," etc. For example:

Twenty	EE-sip
Ninety	KOO-sip

The words for "hundred," "thousand," and "ten thousand," are found only in the Chinese system.

Hundred	PAK
Thousand	*CH*UN
Ten thousand	MAHN

Be sure to notice the difference between the vowel written "a" and the vowel written "ah." The first

U *or* UH *as in* but

is about like our *a* in *pat,* and the second like our *ah* in *bah.*

WHAT'S THIS?

When you want to know the name of something you can say "What's this?" and point to the thing you mean.

What's this?   EE-guss-<u>oo</u>n   moo-uh-SIM-
                            nik-gah?

ASKING FOR THINGS

When you want something, you first name the thing wanted and then add the phrase "Please give me."

Please give me __   __ CHAWM   choo-SIP-
                            see-yaw

  cigarettes   TAHM-ba

Please give me some   TAHM-ba   CHAWM   choo-
  cigarettes   SIP-see-yaw

  matches   SUNG-n'yahng

Please give me some   SUNG-n'yahng   CHAWM
  matches   choo-SIP-see-yaw

Here are the words for some of the things you may require.

food *(in the country)*	MUG-ool GUT
food *(in the city)*	OOM-sik
water	MCOL
eggs	KAY-rahn
soup	KOOK
vegetables	*CH*ASS-aw
meat	KAWG-ee
chicken	TAHK KAWG-ee
fish	SANG-sun
beef	SAW KAWG-ee
pork	TWAJ-ee KAWG-ee
cooked rice	PAHP
potatoes	KAHM-jah
beans	*K*AWNG
cabbage	PACH-hoo
fruit	SIL-gwah
melons	*CH*AH-mer
tea	*CH*AH
milk	OO-yoo

U *or* UH *as in* but

English	Pronunciation
liquor	SOOL
beer	MAK-joo
	or ḄEE-roo
salt	SAW-gawm

MONEY

To find out how much things cost you say really "This costs how much?"

How much does this cost? EE-guss-<u>oo</u>n ul-MAHM-nik-gah?

Kyongbokkung

TIME

To find out what time it is you say really "Now is what time?"

now	CHEE-g<u>oo</u>m
is what time	mess-SIM-nik-gah
What time is it?	CHEE-g<u>oo</u>m mess-SIM-nik-gah?

The hours are counted with the native Korean numbers. For "one o'clock" you say really "one o'clock it is."

one o'clock	HAHN-see
it is	IM-nee-dah

[Note: The most important combinations of numbers and hours, and of numbers and minutes, are given on pages 43-46.]

It's one o'clock	HAHN-see IM-nee-dah
It's two o'clock	TOO-see IM-nee-dah
It's three o'clock	SAY-see IM-nee-dah

For "it's four fifteen" you say really "four o'clock fifteen minutes it is," but the minutes are counted with the Chinese system of numerals.

U *or* UH *as in* but

Tosan-Sa, With Pukhan Mountains In Background

English	Pronunciation
four o'clock	NAY-see
fifteen minutes	SEE-baw-boon
It's four fifteen	NAY-see SEE-baw-boon IM-nee-dah

For "it's four thirty" you say really "four o'clock half it is."

half	PAHN
It's four thirty	NAY-see PAHN IM-nee-dah

For "it's quarter to five" you can say either "four o'clock forty-five minutes it is" or "five o'clock fifteen minutes before it is."

English	Pronunciation
before	CHUN
It's a quarter to five	TAH-suss-see SEE-baw-boon CHUN IM-nee-dah

If you want to know when a movie starts or when a train leaves you say:

movies	HWAHLT-dawng SAH-jin
at what time	MESS-see-ay
do they start	SEE-jahk HAHM-nik-gah
When do the movies start?	HWAHLT-dawng SAH-jin MESS-see-ay SEE-jahk HAHM-nik-gah?
train	KICH-hah
does it leave	ḍuh-NAHM-nik-gah
When does the train leave?	KICH-hah MESS-see-ay ḍuh-NAHM-nik-gah?
Yesterday	UJ-ay
Today	AW-nool
Tomorrow	NA-il

The days of the week are:

Sunday	EER-yaw-il
Monday	WUHR-yaw-il

English	Pronunciation
Tuesday	HWAH-yaw-il
Wednesday	SOO-yaw-il
Thursday	MAWG-yaw-il
Friday	KOOM-yaw-il
Saturday	TAW-yaw-il

OTHER USEFUL PHRASES

The following phrases will be useful.

What is your name?	TAHNG-sin EER-haw-moon moo-uh-SIM-nik-gah?
My name is John	CHAY EER-haw-moon "John"-IM-nee-dah
How do you say "desk" (*or anything else*) in Korean?	"DESK"-rool CHAW-sun MAHL-law moo-UHR-ah-gaw HAHM-nik-gah?
Where is the nearest town?	CHAY-il KAHK-gah-oon TAWNG-nen-oon UDD-et-joom iss-SOOM-nik-gah?
I am an American	NAH-noon MEE-gook sah-RAHM-ee-yaw
Good-by	AHN-n'yung-hee kah-SIP-see-yaw

A *as in* at; AH *as in* bah

ADDITIONAL EXPRESSIONS

English	Pronunciation
I'm hungry	SEE-jahng HAHM-nee-dah
I'm thirsty	MAWNG mah-ROOM-nee-dah
I'm lost	NAH-noon KEE-rool eer-huss-SOOM-nee-dah
I'm sick	NAH-noon CHAWM ahp-HOOM-nee-dah
I'm tired	NAH-noon CHAWM KAW-dahn HAHM-nee-dah
I'm wounded	NAH-noon CHAWM tahch-huss-SOOM-nee-dah
Stop! *(to someone running away)*	KUG-ee SUK-guh-rah
Hold still!	KAH-mah-nee ISS-suh
Wait a minute!	CHAHNG-gahn kee-dah-REE-see-yaw
Come here!	EE-ree AW-see-yaw
Quickly!	ḄAHL-lee
Right away!	KAWT
Come quickly!	ḄAHL-lee AW-see-yaw
Go quickly!	ḄAHL-lee KAH-see-yaw

U *or* UH *as in* but

English	Pronunciation
Help!	SAH-rahm SAHL-l'yoo
Help me	CHAWM TAW-wah choo-SIP-see-yaw
Bring help	SAH-rah mool CHAWM TAHR-yud-ah CHOO-see-yaw
I will pay you	TAWN too-ree-gess-SOOM-nee-dah
I will not forget what you do for me	IT-jee ahn-gess-SOOM-nee-dah

Changdokkung In Winter

English	Pronunciation
Where is it?	UDD-ay iss-SOOM-nik-gah?
Where is the town?	TAWNG-nay-noon UDD-ay iss-SOOM-nik-gah?
How far is the town?	TAWNG-nay GAH-jee UL-mah-nah MUM-nik-gah?
Is it far?	MUM-nik-gah?
How far is it?	UL-mah-nah MUM-nik-gah?
Which way is north?	UN-oo JAWG-ee POOK chaw-GIM-nik-gah?
Which is the road to ___?	UN-oo KEE-ree ___ -oo-raw KAH-noon kee-RIM-nik-gah?
Draw a map for me	CHEE-daw-rool KOOR-yuh CHOO-see-yaw
Take me there	CHAWM TAHR-yud-ah choo-SIP-see-yaw
Take me to a doctor	OO-sah HAHN-day CHAWM TAHR-yud-ah choo-SIP-see-yaw

U *or* UH *as in* but

Tongdaemun - East Gate

English	Pronunciation
Take me to a hospital	P'YUNG-wun-ay CHAWM TAHR-yud-ah choo-SIP-see-yaw
Danger!	WEE-hum HAHM-nee-dah
Watch out!	CHOO-ee HAH-see-yaw
Good-by *(to person staying behind)*	AHN-n'yung-hee keh-SIP-see-yaw
Is it big?	*K*OOM-nik-gah?
It is big	*K*OOM-nee-dah
It is not big	*K*OO-jee ahn-SOOM-nee-dah
Is it good?	chawss-SOOM-nik-gah?
It is good	chawss-SOOM-nee-dah
It is not good	CHAWCH-hee ahn-SOOM-nee-dah

English	Pronunciation
Is it expensive?	piss-SAHM-nik-gah?
It is expensive	piss-SAHM-nee-dah
It is not expensive	PISS-sah-jee ahn-ṢOOM-nee-dah
Is it clean?	ĢAK-goot HAHM-nik-gah?
It is clean	ĢAK-goot HAHM-nee-dah
It is not clean	ĢAK-goot-jee ahn-ṢOOM-nee-dah
Is it near?	kahk-gahp-SOOM-nik-gah?
It is near	kahk-gahp SOOM-nee-dah
It is not near	KAHK-gahp-jee ahn-ṢOOM-nee-dah

FILL-IN SENTENCES

In this section you will find a number of sentences, each containing a blank space which can be filled in with any one of the words in the list that follows. For example, if you want to say "Please give me some soap," find the fill-in sentence "Please give me —" and, in the list following the sentences, the word for "soap." Then combine them as follows:

Please give me __	__ CHAWM choo-SIP-see-yaw
soap	PEE-noo
Please give me some soap	PEE-noo CHAWM choo-SIP-see-yaw

Please give me __	__ CHAWM choo-SIP-see-yaw
Please bring me __	__ CHAWM KAHT-dah choo-SIP-see-yaw
Where is __?	__ UDD-ay iss-SOOM-nik-gah?
I (or we) have __	__ iss-SOOM-nee-dah
I (or we) don't have __	__ up-SOOM-nee-dah
Have you __?	__ iss-SOOM-nik-gah?

A *as in* at; AH *as in* bah

English	Pronunciation
Example:	
Have you ___?	___ iss-S<u>OO</u>M-nik-gah?
noodles	KOOK-soo
Have you noodles?	KOOK-soo iss-S<u>OO</u>M-nik-gah?
barley	PAW-ree
cooked barley	PAW-ree PAHP
food eaten with rice	*CH*AHN
guinea corn	SOO-soo
millet	CHAWP-sahl
cooked millet	CHAWP PAHP
pickled salad	KIM-chee
rice cakes	DUK
soya bean curd	TOO-boo
soya bean sauce	KAHN-jahng
soya bean sprouts	*K*AWNG NAH-mool
white radishes	MOO
a bowl	SAH-bahl
chopsticks	CHUK KAH-rahk
a cup	CHAHN

U *or* UH *as in* but

35

English	Pronunciation
eating utensils	SOO-juh
a glass	YOO-ree CHAHN
a knife	*K*AHL
a plate	CHUP-see
a spoon	SOOK KAH-rahk
a bed	*CH*IM-sahng
blankets	TAHM-n'yaw
a comforter	EE-bool
mosquito net	MAWG-ee CHAHNG
a pillow	P'YUG-a
a room	PAHNG
sheets	HAWN NEE-bool
cigars	KWUL-l'yun
a pipe	KAWM-bahng-da *or* "pipe"
tobacco *or* cigarettes	TAHM-ba
a fountain pen	MAHN-n'yun *P*IL
ink	"ink"
paper	CHAWNG-ee

A *as in* at; AH *as in* bah

English	Pronunciation
a pen	*CH*UL *P*IL
a pencil	YUN *P*IL
a writing brush	POOT
a comb	PEET
hot water	TUH-oon MOOL
a razor	M'YUN-daw
razor blades	M'YUN-daw *K*AHL
soap	PEE-noo
a toothbrush	EE-ṣawl
tooth powder	*CH*EE-yahk
a towel	SAY-soo ṢOO-gun
a handkerchief	SAWN ṢOO-gun
overshoes	TUSS-sin
a raincoat	PEE-awt
rubber-overshoes	KAW-moo TUSS-sin
a shirt	wah-ee-SHAHT-soo
shoelaces	KOO-doo G̣OON
shoe polish	KOO-doo YAHK
shoes	KOO-doo
underwear	SAW-gawt

U *or* UH *as in* but

WHICH IS WHICH?

TOOTHBRUSH

SOAP

EE-sawl
SAY-soo SOO-gun
PEE-noo
M'YUN-daw

TOWEL

RAZOR

(Answers on page 37)

English	Pronunciation
buttons	TAHNCH-hoo
a needle	PAH˛nool
safety pins	"pin"
thread	SEEL
aspirin	"aspirin"
a bandage	POONG-da
cotton	SAWM
a disinfectant	SAW-dawk CHAY
a laxative	P'YUN-bee JAY
gasoline	"gasoline"

I want to __	NAH-noon __ -gaw sip-HOOM-nee-dah
Example:	
I want to __	NAH-noon __ -gaw sip-HOOM-nee-dah
eat	MUK-
I want to eat	NAH-noon MUK-gaw sip-HOOM-nee-dah
drink *(water)*	MOOL MUK-

U *or* UH *as in* but

English	Pronunciation
have a haircut	EE-bahl HAH-
rest	SHWEE-
shave	M'YUN-daw HAH-
sleep	CHAH-
wash my face	SAY-soo HAH-

Where is a ___? *or* Where is the ___?	___ UDD-ay iss-SOOM-nik-gah?

Example:

Where is a ___?	___ UDD-ay iss-SOOM-nik-gah?
barber shop	EE-bahl SAW
Where is a barber shop?	EE-bahl SAW UDD-ay iss-SOOM-nik-gah?
doctor	OO-sah
servant	HAH-in
policeman	SOON-sah
shoemaker	KOO-doo ḄAHNG
tailor	YAHNG-bawk JUM
bridge	TAH-ree

A *as in* at; AH *as in* bah

English	Pronunciation
bus	BUSS-soo
camp	CHUN-mahk
church	YEB-a TAHNG
house	CHIP
laundry	SET-hahk SAW
market	SEE-jahng *or* CHUJ-ah
post office	OOP-h'yun KOOK
railroad	CHUL-law
river	KAHNG
road	KIL
school	HAHK-g'yaw
streetcar	CHUN-chah
telephone	CHUN-hwah
well	OO-mool

WHICH IS WHICH?

BRIDGE

BANDAGE

CHUN-hwah
TAH-ree
POONG-da
KICH-hah

TRAIN

TELEPHONE

(Answers in Word List)

EXPRESSIONS WITH NUMBERS

Numbers and words like "EE" ("Chinese mile"), "CHUN" and "WUN" (Korean money), "POON" ("minute") and "SEE" ("o'clock") change form when put together. The most important combinations are given in the following section.

CHINESE NUMBERS

1	IL	11	SIB-il	10	SIP
2	EE	12	SIB-ee	20	EE-sip
3	SAHM	13	SIP-sahm	30	SAHM-sip
4	SAH	14	SIP-sah	40	SAH-sip
5	AW	15	SIB-aw	50	AW-sip
6	YOOK	16	SIM-n'yook	60	YOOK-sip
7	*CH*IL	17	SIP-*chi*l	70	*CH*IL-sip
8	*P*AHL	18	SIP-hahl	80	*P*AHL-sip
9	KOO	19	SIP-goo	90	KOO-sip
10	SIP				

100	PAK
1,000	*CH*UN
10,000	MAHN

Amounts of Money with Chinese Numbers

Number	CHUN	WUN (100 CHUN)
1	IL-jun	EER-wun
2	EE-jun	EE-wun
3	SAHM-jun	SAHM-wun
4	SAH-jun	SAH-wun
5	AW-jun	AW-wun
6	YOOK-jun	YOOG-wun
7	CHIL-jun	CHEER-wun
8	PAHL-jun	PAHR-wun
9	KOO-jun	KOO-wun
10	SIP-jun	SIB-wun
100	PAK-jun	PAG-wun
1,000		CHUN-wun

Other Combinations

Number	Chinese Miles (EE)	Minutes (POON)
1	IL-lee	IL-boon
2	EE-ree	EE-boon
3	SAHM-nee	SAHM-boon
4	SAH-ree	SAH-boon
5	AW-ree	AW-boon
6	YOONG-nee	YOOK-boon
7	CHIL-lee	CHIL-boon
8	PAHL-lee	PAHL-boon
9	KOO-ree	KOO-boon
10	SIM-nee	SIP-boon
100	PANG-nee	
1,000	CHUL-lee	

A *as in* at; AH *as in* bah

You will notice that to say "seventeen" you say "ten-seven," and that to say "seven miles," you say "seven mile," with a little change as the words are run together. To say "seventeen miles" you say simply "ten-seven-mile," and make all the changes, as the words are run together, that are indicated in the above tables; so that the form is "SIP-*ch*il-lee." Similarly, to say "eighteen WUN" you say "ten-eight-WUN" with the changes indicated, giving "SIP-hah-wun." The only exception to this is the expression for "fifteen miles," which is sometimes said "SEE-aw-ree" instead of "SIB-aw-ree."

NATIVE KOREAN NUMBERS

1	HAH-nah	11	YUHR-hah-nah	10	YUL
2	TOOL	12	YUL-dool	20	SOO-mool
3	SET	13	YUL-set	30	SUH-roon
4	NET	14	YUL-let	40	MAH-hoon
5	TAH-sut	15	YUL-dah-sut	50	SHWIN
6	YUSS-ut	16	YUHR-yuss-ut	60	YAY-shwin
7	IL-gawp	17	YUHR-il-gawp	70	EE-roon
8	YUD-ul	18	YUHR-yud-ul	80	YUD-oon
9	AH-hawp	19	YUHR-ah-hawp	90	AH-hoon
10	YUL				

U *or* UH *as in* but

EXPRESSIONS OF TIME

English	Pronunciation
one o'clock	HAHN-see
two o'clock	TOO-see
three o'clock	SAY-see
four o'clock	NAY-see
five o'clock	TAH-suss-see
six o'clock	YUSS-uss-see
seven o'clock	IL-gawp-see
eight o'clock	YUD-ul-see
nine o'clock	AH-hawp-see
ten o'clock	YUL-see
eleven o'clock	YUHR-hahn-see
twelve o'clock	YUL-doo-see

A *as in* at; AH *as in* bah

IMPORTANT SIGNS

English	Korean	Chinese
STOP	정지	停止
GO SLOW	천천히가시요	徐行
CAUTION	주의	注意
DANGER	위험	危險
NO THOROUGHFARE	통행금지	通行禁止
DEAD END	막다른골목	
KEEP TO THE LEFT	좌측통행	左側通行
DANGEROUS; GO SLOW	위험서형	危險徐行

Soraksan National Park

English	*Korean*	*Chinese*
RAILROAD	기차시걸	汽車鐵路
BRIDGE	다.리	橋
MEN	남자변소	男子便所
WOMEN	여자변소	女子便所
LAVATORY	변소	便所
NO SMOKING	담배피지마시요	禁煙
NO SPITTING	침뱉지마시요	
KEEP OUT	일없는사람들어오지마시요	閒人勿入

Kyongbok Palace On New Years Day

Chollabuk-Do - Namwon

49

Kangwon-Do - Village On East Coast

ALPHABETICAL WORD LIST

Korean words frequently change form when put together into sentences. Thus the word for "soldier" is "P'YUNG-jung," but in the sentence "Where are the soldiers?" the word has the form "p'yung-JUNG-doo-roon": "p'yung-JUNG-doo-roon UDD-ay iss-SOOM-nik-gah?" These changes also take place when numbers are used with words like "SEE" ("o'clock"). The numbers and combinations with them are given on pages 43-46, and are not included in the ALPHABETICAL WORD LIST.

English	Pronunciation
A	
American	MEE-gook
I am an American	NAH-n<u>oo</u>n MEE-gook sah-RAH-mee-yaw
American soldier	MEE-gook P'YUNG-jung
aspirin	"aspirin"
B	
bandage	POONG-da
barber shop	EE-bahl SAW

U *or* UH *as in* but

English	Pronunciation
barley	PAW-ree
cooked barley	PAW-ree PAHP
beans	*K*AWNG
soya bean curd	TOO-boo
soya bean sauce	KAHN-jahng
soya bean sprouts	*K*AWNG NAH-mool
bed	*CH*IM-sahng
beef	SAW KAWG-ee
beer	MAK-joo
	or BEE-roo
big	
Is it big?	*K*OOM-nik-gah?
It is big	*K*OOM-nee-dah
It is not big	*K*OO-jee ahn-ṢOOM-nee-dah
blades	
razor blades	M'YUN-daw *K*AHL
blankets	TAHM-n'yaw
bowl	SAH-bahl
bridge	TAH-ree

A *as in* at; AH *as in* bah

English	*Pronunciation*
bring	
Bring help	SAH-rah-mool CHAWM TAHR-yud-ah CHOO-see-yaw
Please bring me ___	___ CHAWM KAHT-dah choo-SIP-see-yaw
bus	BUSS-soo
buttons	TAHNCH-hoo

C

cabbage	PACH-hoo
camp	*CH*UN-mahk
chicken	TAHK KAWG-ee
chopsticks	CHUK KAH-rahk
church	YEB-a TAHNG

Kyongsangbuk - Pottery Kiln

English	Pronunciation
cigarettes	TAHM-ba
Please give me some cigarettes	TAHM-ba CHAWM choo-SIP-see-yaw
cigars	KWUL-l'yun
clean	
Is it clean?	ĠAK-goot HAHM-nik-gah?
It is clean	ĠAK-goot HAHM-nee-dah
It is not clean	ĠAK-goot-jee ahn-ṢOOM-nee-dah
comb	PIT

Seoul - Ungam-Dong

English	Pronunciation
come	
Come here!	EE-ree AW-see-yaw
Come quickly!	BAHL-lee AW-see-yaw
comforter	EE-bool
cost	
How much does this cost?	EE-guss-<u>oo</u>n ul-MAHM-nik-gah?
This costs two "CHUN"	EE-guss-<u>oo</u>n EE-jun chah-RIM-nee-dah
cotton	SAWM
cup	CHAHN

D

Danger!	WEE-hum HAHM-nee-dah
disinfectant	SAW-dawk CHAY
doctor	<u>OO</u>-sah
Take me to a doctor	<u>OO</u>-sah HAHN-day CHAWM TAHR-yud-ah choo-SIP-see-aw
drink	
I want to drink (water)	NAH-n<u>oo</u>n MOOL MUK-gaw sip-H<u>OO</u>M-nee-dah

English	Pronunciation

E

eat

    I want to eat — NAH-n<u>oo</u>n MUK-gaw sip-H<u>OO</u>M-nee-dah

eating utensils — SOO-juh

eggs — KAY-rahn

excuse

    Please excuse me — YAWNG-suh hah-SIP-see-yaw

expensive

    Is it expensive? — piss-SAHM-nik-gah?

    It is expensive — piss-SAHM-nee-dah

    It is not expensive — PISS-sah-jee ahn-S<u>OO</u>M-nee-dah

F

far

    How far is it? — UL-mah-nah MUM-nik-gah?

    How far is the town? — TAWNG-nay ĢAH-jee UL-mah-nah MUM-nik-gah?

A *as in* at; AH *as in* bah

Pukhansan National Park - Painting on Sungga Temple

Kyongsangbuk-Do - Ship Launching

English	Pronunciation
Is it far?	MUM-nik-gah?
fish	SANG-sun
food	
in the country	MUG-<u>oo</u>l GUT
in the city	<u>OO</u>M-sik
fountain pen	MAHN-n'yun *PIL*
Friday	*K*<u>OO</u>M-yaw-il
fruit	SIL-gwah

G

gasoline	"gasoline"
give	
Please give me ___	___ CHAWN choo-SIP-see-yaw
glass	YOO-ree CHAHN
go	
Go quickly!	BAHL-lee KAH-see-yaw
Go straight ahead	AHP-h<u>oo</u>-raw KAWT-jahng kah-SIP-see-yaw
Go this way	EE-ree kah-SIP-see-yaw

English	Pronunciation
good	
Is it good?	chawss-S<u>OO</u>M-nik-gah?
It is good	chawss-S<u>OO</u>M-nee-dah
It is not good	CHAWCH-hee ahn-S<u>OO</u>M-nee-dah
Good-by *(to person leaving)*	AHN-n'yung-hee kah-SIP-see-yaw
Good-by *(to person staying behind)*	AHN-n'yung-hee keh-SIP-see-yaw
guinea corn	SOO-soo

H

haircut	
I want to have a haircut	NAH-n<u>oo</u>n EE-bahl HAH-gaw sip-H<u>OO</u>M-nee-dah
half	PAHN
handkerchief	SAWN ŞOO-gun
have	
Have you ___?	___ iss-S<u>OO</u>M-nik-gah?
I (we) don't have ___	___ up-S<u>OO</u>M-nee-dah
I (we) have ___	___ iss-S<u>OO</u>M-nee-dah

A *as in* at; AH *as in* bah

English	Pronunciation

Help! — SAH-rahm SAHL-l'yoo

Help me — CHAWM TAW-wah choo-SIP-see-yaw

Bring help — SAH-rah-mool CHAWM TAHR-yud-ah CHOO-see-yaw

here

Come here! — EE-ree AW-see-yaw

hour *(See pages 25 and 43-46.)* — SEE

hospital — P'YUNG-wun

Take me to a hospital — P'YUNG-wun-ay CHAWM TAHR-yud-ah choo-SIP-see-yaw

hotel — YUG-wahn

Where is a hotel? — YUG-wahn-oon UDD-ay iss-SOOM-nik-gah?

house — CHIP

how

How do you say "desk" in Korean? — "DESK"-rool CHAW-sun MAHL-law moo-UL-ah-gaw HAHM-nik-gah?

How much does this cost? — EE-guss-oon ul-MAHM-nik-gah?

U *or* UH *as in* but   **59**

English	Pronunciation
How do you do?	AHN-n'yung hah-SIM-nik-gah?
How far is it?	UL-mah-nah MUM-nik-gah?
How far is the town?	TAWNG-nay ĢAH-jee UL-mah-nah MUM-nik-gah?
hungry	
I am hungry	SEE-jahng HAHM-nee-dah

I

I	NAH-n<u>oo</u>n
I don't have ___	___ up-S<u>OO</u>M-nee-dah
I have ___	___ iss-S<u>OO</u>M-nee-dah
I want to ___	NAH-n<u>oo</u>n ___ -gaw sip-H<u>OO</u>M-nee-dah
ink	"ink"

K

knife	KAHL

L

laundry	SET-hahk SAW

A *as in* at; AH *as in* bah

WHICH IS WHICH?

FRUIT

HOUSE

SIL-gwah
KAY-rahn
CHIP
KAHL

KNIFE

EGGS

(Answers in Word List)

English	Pronunciation
laxative	P'YUN-bee JAY
leave	
When does the train leave?	KICH-hah MESS-see-ay duh-NAHM-nik-gah?
left	
It is to the left	ERN JAW-gay iss-SOOM-nee-dah
liquor	SOOL
lost	
I am lost	NAH-noon KEE-rool eer-huss-SOOM-nee-dah

M

English	Pronunciation
madam	POO-in
map	CHEE-daw
Draw a map for me	CHEE-daw-rool KOOR-yuh CHOO-see-yaw
market	SEE-jahng
	or CHUJ-ah
matches	SUNG-n'yahng
meat	KAWG-ee
melons	*CH*AH-mer

English	Pronunciation
mile *(Chinese; see page 44.)*	EE
milk	OO-yoo
millet	CHAWP-sahl
cooked millet	CHAW PAHP
minute *(See page 44.)*	POON
Wait a minute!	CHAHNG-gahn kee-dah-REE-see-yaw
Miss	YAHNG
Monday	WUHR-yaw-il
mosquito net	MAWG-ee CHAHNG
movies	HWAHLT-dawng SAH-jin
When do the movies start?	HWAHLT-dawng SAH-jin MESS-see-ay SEE-jahk HAHM-nik-gah?
Mr.	SUN-sang
Mrs.	POO-in

Yi Dynasty Farmhouse Near Andong

English	Pronunciation

N

name	EER-hawn
My name is John	CHAY EER-haw-m<u>oo</u>n "John"-IM-nee-dah
What is your name?	TAHNG-sin EER-haw-m<u>oo</u>n moo-uh-SIM-nik-gah?
near	
Is it near?	kahk-gahp-S<u>OO</u>M-nik-gah?
It is near	kahk-gahp-S<u>OO</u>M-nee-dah
It is not near	KAHK-gahp-jee ahn-Ṣ<u>OO</u>M-nee-dah
needle	PAH-nool
no	AH-nee-yaw
north	
Which way is north?	UN-<u>oo</u> JAWG-ee POOK chaw-K̄IM-nik-gah?
now	CHEE-g<u>oo</u>m

O

o'clock *(See page 46.)*	SEE
overshoes	TUSS-sin
rubber overshoes	KAW-moo TUSS-sin

A *as in* at; AH *as in* bah

Changdokkung - Changdok Palace

Cheju-Do - Tolharubang (grandfather image)

English	Pronunciation

P

English	Pronunciation
paper	CHAWNG-ee
pay	
I will pay you	TAWN too-ree-gess-SOOM-nee-dah
pen	*CH*UL *P*IL
fountain pen	MAHN-n'yun *P*IL
pencil	YUN *P*IL
pillow	P'YUG-a
pin	
safety pin	"pin"
pipe	KAWM-bahng-da *or* "pipe"
plate	CHUP-see
please	CHAWM

[NOTE: "CHAWM" really means "a little bit." It is often used where we use "please" in a sentence, but is not used as a whole sentence by itself.]

Please point	CHAWM KAH-rooch-huh choo-SIP-see-yaw
policeman	SOON-sah

English	Pronunciation
English	*Pronunciation*

polish

    shoe polish KOO-doo YAHK

pork TWAJ-ee KAWG-ee

post office OOP-h'yun KOOK

potatoes KAHM-jah

Q

quarter

    It is a quarter past four NAY-see SEE-baw-boon IM-nee-dah

    It is a quarter to five TAH-suss-see SEE-baw-boon CHUN IM-nee-dah

question

    May I ask a question? MAHL-ṣoom CHAWM MOO-ruh PAWP-see-dah

Kyongbokkung Subway Station

English	Pronunciation
Quickly!	BAHL-lee
Come quickly!	BAHL-lee AW-see-yaw
Go quickly!	BAHL-lee KAH-see-yaw

R

English	Pronunciation
radishes	
white radishes	MOO
railroad	*CH*UL-law
railroad station	CHUNG-guh CHAHNG
Where is the railroad station?	CHUNG-guh CHAHNG-oon UDD-ay iss-S<u>OO</u>M-nık-gah?
raincoat	PEE-awt
razor	M'YUN-daw
razor blades	M'YUN-daw *KAHL*
repeat	
Please repeat	CHAWM TAH-see MAHL-ṣ<u>oo</u>m hah-SIP-see-yaw
rest	
I want to rest	NAH-n<u>oo</u>n SHWEE-gaw sip-H<u>OO</u>M-nee-dah

U *or* UH *as in* but

English	Pronunciation
restaurant	OOM-sik-jum
Where is a restaurant?	oom-SIK-jum-oon UDD-ay iss-SOOM-nik-gah?
rice	
cooked rice	PAHP
rice cakes	DUK
right	
It is to the right	PAH-roon JAW-gay iss-SOOM-nee-dah
Right away!	KAWT
river	KAHNG
road	KIL
Which is the road to ___?	UN-oo KEE-ree ___-oo raw KAH-noon kee-RIM-nik-gah?
room	PAHNG

S

salt	SAW-gawm
Saturday	TAW-yaw-il
school	HAHK-g'yaw
servant	HAH-een

　　　A *as in* at; AH *as in* bah

WHICH IS WHICH?

PLATE

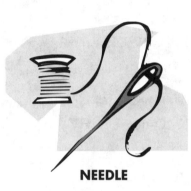

NEEDLE

CHUP-see
YUN *PIL*
PAH-nool
P'YUN-saw

PENCIL

TOILET

(Answers in Word List)

English	Pronunciation
shave	
I want to shave	NAH-noon M'YUN-daw HAH-gaw sip-HOOM-nee-dah
sheets	HAWN NEE-bool
shirt	wah-ee-SHAHT-soo
shoelaces	KOO-doo GOON
shoemaker	KOO-doo BAHNG
shoe polish	KOO-doo YAHK
shoes	KOO-doo
sick	
I am sick	NAH-noon CHAWM ahp-HOOM-nee-dah
sir	SUN-sang
sleep	
I want to sleep	NAH-noon CHAH-gaw sip-HOOM-nee-dah
slowly	*CH*UN-*ch*un-hee
Please speak slowly	CHAWM *CH*UN-*ch*un-hee MAHL-soom hah-SIP-see-yaw
soap	PEE-noo

A *as in* at; AH *as in* bah

English	Pronunciation
soldiers	P'YUNG-jung
soup	KOOK
speak	
Please speak slowly	CHAWM *CH*UN-*ch*un-hee MAHL-ṣ<u>oo</u>m hah-SIP-see-yaw
spoon	SOOK KAH-rahk
start	
When do the movies start?	HWAHLT-dawng SAH-jin MESS-see-ay SEE-jahk HAHM-nik-gah?
station	
railroad station	CHUNG-guh CHAHNG
Stop! *(to someone running away)*	KUG-ee SUK-guh-rah
streetcar	CHUN-*ch*ah
Sunday	EER-yaw-il

English	Pronunciation
	T
tailor	YAHNG-bawk JUM
take	
Take me there	CHAWM TAHR-yud-ah choo-SIP-see-yaw
Take me to a doctor	OO-sah HAHN-day CHAWM TAHR-yuh-ah choo-SIP-see-yaw
Take me to a hospital	P'YUNG-wun-ay CHAWM TAHR-yud-ah choo-SIP-see-yaw
tea	CHAH
telephone	CHUN-hwah
Thank you	kaw-mahp-SOOM-nee-dah
there	
Take me there	CHAWM TAHR-yud-ah choo-SIP-see-yaw
thirsty	
I'm thirsty	MAWNG mah-ROOM-nee-dah
this	EE-gut
What is this?	EE-guss-oon moo-uh-SIM-nik-gah?

English	Pronunciation
thread	SEEL
Thursday	MAWG-yaw-il
time *(See pages 25-27 and 43-46.)*	
What time is it?	CHEE-g<u>oo</u>m mess-SIM nik-gah?
tired	
I am tired	NAH-n<u>oo</u>n CHAWM KAW-dahn HAHM-nee-dah
tobacco	TAHM-ba
today	AW-n<u>oo</u>l
toilet	P'YUN-saw
Where is a toilet?	P'YUN-saw-n<u>oo</u>n UDD-ay iss-S<u>OO</u>M-nik-gah?
tomorrow	NA-il
toothbrush	EE-ṣawl
tooth powder	*CH*EE-yahk
towel	SAY-soo ṢOO-gun
town	TAWNG-nay
Where is the nearest town?	CHAY-il KAHK-gah-oon TAWNG-nen-<u>oo</u>n UDD-et-j<u>oo</u>m iss-S<u>OO</u>M-nik-gah?

U *or* UH *as in* but   **73**

WHICH IS WHICH?

SHOES

SPOON

SAW-gawm
CHAH
SOOK KAH-rahk
KOO-doo

SALT

TEA

(Answers in Word List)

English	Pronunciation
Where is the town?	TAWNG-nay-noon UDD-ay iss-SOOM-nik-gah?
train	KICH-hah
When does the train leave?	KICH-hah MESS-see-ay duh-NAHM-nik-gah?
Tuesday	HWAH-yaw-il

U

understand	
Do you understand me?	AH-rah took-gess-SOOM-nik-gah?
I don't understand	CHAHL maw-roo-gess-SOOM-nee-dah
I understand	AH-rah took-gess-SOOM-nee-dah
underwear	SAW-gawt

V

vegetables	CHASS-aw

W

Wait a minute!	CHAHNG-gahn kee-dah-REE-see-yaw

U *or* UH *as in* but

Pukhansan National Park

English	Pronunciation
wash	
I want to wash my face	NAH-noon SAY-soo HAH-gaw sip-HOOM-nee-dah
Watch out!	CHOO-ee HAH-see-yaw
water	MOOL
hot water	TUH-oon MOOL
Wednesday	SOO-yaw-il
we	
we don't have ___	___ up-SOOM-nee-dah
We have ___	___ iss-SOOM-nee-dah
well *(for water)*	OO-mool
what	MOO-ut
What is this?	EE-guss-oon moo-uh-SIM-nik-gah?
What is your name?	TAHNG-sin EER-haw-moon moo-uh-SIM-nik-gah?
What time is it?	CHEE-goom mess-SIM-nik-gah?
where	UDD-ay
Where is a (*or* the) ___?	___ UDD-ay iss-SOOM-nik-gah?

English	Pronunciation
which	UN-<u>oo</u>
Which is the road to __?	UN-<u>oo</u> KEE-ree __ -<u>oo</u>-raw KAH-n<u>oo</u>n kee-RIM-nik-gah?
Which way is north?	UN-<u>oo</u> JAWG-ee POOK chaw-GIM-nik-gah?
wounded	
I am wounded	NAH-n<u>oo</u>n CHAWM tahch-huss-S<u>OO</u>M-nee-dah
writing brush	POOT

Y

yes	YAY
yesterday	ÜJ-ay